Superbloom

MAKAELA SMITH

Bainbridge Island Press

Super

MAKAELA SMITH

Bainbridge Island Press

Bainbridge Island, WA

Published in 2024 by Bainbridge Island Press
Bainbridge Island, WA
https://bainbridgeisland.press

Printed in the United States of America

ISBN: 978-1-961451-05-6
Library of Congress Control Number: 2024932708

Cover & Book Design: Ben Rockwood

9 8 7 6 5 4 3 2 1

to my love, Alex, for his inspiration

to my parents for their support

*and to my younger self who never thought she
would make it this far*

Acknowledgements

The following poems can also be found other collections:

"The Island Who Wants To Be The Sea"
Ode to Summer
BookLeaf Publishing

"Summer's Advice"
Ode to Summer
BookLeaf Publishing

Contents

Drought

Monsoon

Superbloom

Superbloom

MAKAELA SMITH

Drought

Desertification

I weave / My feet
Into / The terrain

My body / Bends
Into / A root

Reaching / Down
Through / Desert dust

My arms / Branch out /
To a cloudless sky /
With aimless, precipitous lust /

My tongue / Sunbathes /
Aching for a taste /
Of torrential rain /

I tell myself
It will come again /
One day /
One day.

Virga

Occasionally,
In the desert,
There is rainfall
That never reaches
The ground —

Just when
The sand blossom
Thought
She was going
To savor
One last drop
Before facing
The drought —

The syrup drips
From the sky
And misses her tongue.

Desertare (the Latin root)

I have become
One with the sand

An ocean
Abandoned

A land
Forsaken

A place known by all for
Lacking something

Whether it be rainfall,
Fertile soil,

Or grace.

Saguaro Cactus Blossom

Ever-stretching fingertips
Searching the sultry summer sky

For a white-winged dove
Or a desert orangetip butterfly

To pollinate my wild flowers
Quickly running out of time

My arms — out — like a saguaro cactus
Begging for its life

I only have twenty-four hours
And I have wasted half of my time
Waiting all of last night
For a long-tongued bat
Who never came

Maybe it's time I give up on bearing fruit
And give my arms
A rest in the shade.

Inner Coyotes

Come in,
Please,

Slip off your claws,

And enter into
The desert
Of my mind,

If you dare
Cross paths
With the rest of my pack

Who guard
My hollow heart

Like their den
In the dead of night.

Carousel

The Devil's Playground
Once offered sanctuary
To all of the desert's creatures

Now a barren
Ring of salt

Is all that remains
Of a carousel
Long lost.

An Only Child

I only find myself
When I am lost

In the wilderness
I am wild

Wolfberry juice
Stains the corners
Of my mouth
Like blood

I tuck myself in-
to dead
Flowerbeds

In the familial universe
I am an only child.

A Letter to the Snow

I know you're out there / on the highest mountain peaks / melting on someone else's tongue / revealing your ivory skin / to the eavesdropping evergreens / while I am drowning here / in heat waves / that have begun / to look like the sea / making snow angels / in quicksand / that no one will ever see.

Broken Seal

Deep down
I'm a runaway
Too afraid
To run away

I am
A full moon
Too insecure
To show her face

I say
I look forward
To the future
But I am
Averting my gaze

I wander
Through Death Valley
Carrying an open letter
Addressed to myself

Too afraid
To seal my fate.

Dormant Seeds

Maybe I
Was never meant
To fit in
With the rest

Never meant
To go out
To house parties
Or to prom
Or have a best friend

Never trusting enough
To rise above the dust

Never the flower
To make the first move
And kiss the Sun.

Forbidden Fruit

Rattlesnakes
Are charming,

But please,
Pay no mind

To the desert predators
With hidden venom
Stored behind
Inviting eyes;

I have fallen prey
Far too many times,

So I can only hope
You heed my advice —
Forbidden fruit
May taste sweet
During the initial bite,

But in the end,
You must decide
If it's worth
The mortal fall
From paradise.

As Above, So Below

The landscape
Of his poetry
Was the desert

He always kept
His oasis
Tucked away
For himself

But I know
Six feet below
The rivers run clear

I remember
Six years ago
He had brought me here

And for six nights
He made hell
Feel just like home

As we swam through Lethe together

But he claims he doesn't remember

He says there's never been a river.

Flood Watch

The veins
In my leaves
Have grown
So tired

From carrying
The weight
Of the world's
Carnivorous desires

Maybe it's time
I open up
And spill
Some blood

But I worry
This desert soil
May be too shallow
To retain a running river —
Let alone survive a flash flood.

Desperate/Desolate

I'm not afraid
Of being lost
In the desert

Desperate
And desolate

Dehydrated
Drenched in sweat

I'm afraid
Of finding
The oasis
I've been searching for
And finally seeing my reflection
In the pool

And not liking who I see looking back

Not liking what I have become.

Snake Pit

Let me out
Of my mind

It's not safe
Here inside

I see silhouettes slither by
Like serpents in the night

Then disintegrate
The moment
I turn on the light.

War/den

My own garden walls
Hold me back

I thought they stood strong
To keep me safe

But my fortress
Is under attack

I forgot
My worst enemy

Has been my own thorns
Since the beginning.

Brave/heart

The brave heart
Of our Earth
Is breaking

And we are here
Skinny dipping
In her tears

Look —
Her emerald city
Is burning

But no one
Is willing
To risk their skin
To interfere

We just keep on
Feeding fires
With our fear

Pouring gasoline
Into seas

Begging skies
To grow clear.

Goddess Letters

Goddess of Earth,
My head has been
Uncharted in the clouds,
But I ache to root my feet in your ground.

Goddess of Water,
My home has always been
Boarded up from the inside,
But I would welcome you in like the tide.

Goddess of Fire,
My chest has long been
An underground chamber with no light,
But I think it's time for our flame to ignite.

Goddess of Air,
I have been clutching
My own throat,
Choking on my own smoke,
And you have made me aware —

None of you
Can save me

Only reveal
What is already there.

Rain Shadow

I chose
To root myself
In the rain shadow

Nobody forced me —

Peace
Has always been
Within my
        reach

And I am the only mountain range
Still standing — in between —
Living in a drought
And living out my dreams.

Lethe, River of Oblivion

I crawl out of
The cave of Hypnos

        Vulnerable, but prepared

My mouth waters for
The river of Lethe

        Speeding toward oblivion, but aware

Bare,
Rose petal skin
        Laid out
                For the burn of acid rain

I am ready
        To be hurt
                Again.

A Letter to the Rain

I think it's time that you came and stayed.
I'm sorry I always used to push you away.
That's so like me.

Proximity

I stood out
In the open
Awaiting a thunderstorm

And you were
The first
Raindrop
To hit me.

Silver Linings

I don't think storms are named after people anymore/
I think people are named after storms/ And I have
a sense that your name is up next/ Because I nev-
er used to like going out in the rain/ But I've been
standing out in my driveway for days/ Awaiting your
hurricane/ Where I imagine falling asleep to your
thunder each night/ I already feel your lightning in
my dreams/ And I envision waking up to your calm
every morning/ Where your lips will be my silver
linings/ And the sun will shine/ Like blush through
your cheeks.

Monsoon

Summer's Advice

Don't be afraid
To go out
In the storm

Don't be afraid
To become it.

Relief

The waterfall
And her mist

They're coming
To introduce me

To all of the beauty
I have missed

While depression
Held down my feet

There are far too many gardens
I have yet to see

And there are entire oceans
Left to explore

I have merely stood on the beach.

Curiouser

I held no fear in my chest
As I stepped out into the sea

It was the untold mystery
Of the shadows swimming beneath

That hypnotized my feet
Like the Greek god of sleep

From the moment I was born
I knew curiosity
Would mean certain death to me

But I was still willing
To let the ocean take me
Down at the shore
Begging on my knees

Honestly, I would do anything
To feel
Anything

So for you, I pretend I can walk on water —

I pretend I will never look back to the beach.

Rain Drunk

I am covered
In flaws
And freckles
And self-made torrential rain

I am a mess
And undressed
And vulnerable to pain

But I say I like it this way
And I make the choice
To invite you to stay

Hey, tonight,
Why don't you come over
And open up
My mouth?
I've been stranded in the desert for days

In moments,
You came running
Carrying a bottle
Of the most expensive champagne

Already opened,
Pouring out all over the driveway.

Flowerbed

Your vines
Spiral
And wrap themselves
Around
My ankles and wrists

Holding me down
Against the flowerbed

Your fingertips
Like thorns
Slowly growing
Into my throat.

Brontë

Goddess of thunder
Commander of lightning

Within your prying eyes
I see storm clouds spiraling

When I first
Stepped outside
You were
A light rain

Until overnight
You became
Catastrophic
To my terrain.

Rip Current

The Sun and The Moon
Both pull at my seams

Everyday I am caught
In a reoccurring rip current dream

And I can never remember
Which way to swim to break free

The only escape now
Is allowing the sea
To purposely
Drown me.

Desert Wallflower

The dandelion thrived
Throughout
The monsoon
And the drought

But the desert wallflower
On the other hand
Drowned
In the undertow
Of self-doubt

She believed
She couldn't

And so she never
Made it out.

Lovesong

Spotlight on the surface
Of your sea

All can see
Your ball gown
Aquamarine and glittering

Your fragile fabric
Rippling in the breeze

The full moon
Composing sweet, sedating melodies

Violin strings
Singing love notes
We were never eloquent enough to speak

And just before the clock strikes twelve
You ask to dance with me —
Of course, I said yes,
I wanted a Cinderella story —

If only your pressure
Wasn't slowly killing me

If only this romance
Wasn't fantasy.

Morning Glory

With climbing vines
Wrapped tight
Around my mind

The air had grown
Far too toxic
For your ivory flowers
To thrive outside

So they forced their way in
And I said it was fine

My fire had faded —
Body too weak to put up a fight.

Toxins

I thought you were
Supposed to be
My cure

I didn't know
It was you
Who had slipped
The poison
Into my glass
Long ago

Before so kindly
Introducing me
To your antidote.

Wilting

You let me
Rot away

Forgotten on the top shelf
In a cracked glass vase

Perfectly placed

Just out of reach

Of the Sun's rays.

Green Envy

You were always
In envy
Of the cherry blossom trees

And the way
Their falling petals
Would flirt with me

Play with my hair
And brush against my cheek

And the way
The sunlight
Could touch my skin

With a warmth
You never could

The Earth and I
Had fallen deeply in love

In a way
I knew
We never would.

Lost Signal

In the silence
In the distance
In the mist

I can see the green light
At the end
Of someone's dock

Across from me
Across the world
Across the sea

I'll be
Here
For them

                                        But they
                                   Won't hear
                                   From me

        Both of us are calling for each other's help

Just out of

                            reach.

Double-Edged Thorn

Your thorns

        Caught

In my fingertips

My heart

        Trapped

Behind your ribs

Blood drips down
        From both of our hands

But we can no longer tell
        Whose rain it is

Now we have bloodstains
All over our brand-new carpet
And we both
Blame the other for it.

Ribbon Lightning

A heart / Beating / Down / On our skylight
Ribbon lightning / Reflected
In two gray eyes

Blue blackout curtains / Pushed off to one side
In hopes the eye / Of the storm
Might peer in / To empathize

As torrential rain / Pounds down now
Onto my bare / Shivering thighs

Windows / And doors
/Both bolted
From the inside\

Two / Closed / Minds.

Lost Sight

My tongue
                    Was
Twisted
            Into
Torrential
                    Lies

Your thumbs
                    Were
Pressed deep
                    Into
My eyes

I lost
        Sight
Of   myself
        Late
Last   night

And I may never see
That version of me
                    Again in this life.

Somewhere

I know the Sun is shining

                                           Somewhere

The rivers are running
The clouds are parting
The lilies are blooming

                                           Somewhere

In my dreams I am

                                                  There

Still the rain keeps pouring

                                Here

The ravines are filling
The storm clouds are spiraling
The streets are flooding

                                Here

In reality, I will always be

                                Here.

Fading

Release your grip
On her stem

The blush
Has begun
To leave
Her petals

Instead of painting
The roses red

You seem to enjoy
Draining roses
Of their color.

Dripping

Where is your heart?
                    Well, have you checked my sleeve?

                                        I left it open
                                        And bleeding
                          In hopes that you might see

But you kept
Your eyes closed,
Only stirring slightly
In your sleep

                              But my scars are still
                                        Dripping
                          Onto the sugar sand
                                Beneath my feet
            I try to explain,
      But you lift your finger
                To my lips
                And say,
            "Don't speak."

Holding Hands

They tell me
It's spring
But my hands
Are ice cold

You don't hold me
The way you used to anymore

Your limp fingers
Lie dead
Between mine

And you call it
A display of affection

I call it
Pretending to be alive.

The Monsoon

I let
The monsoon
Ruin
My home

I can't blame
The roof
Or the walls
Or the trees
That crashed into them

In the end,
It was my integrity
That wasn't strong enough
To hold up.

Amber Dust

You helped me / weld a cage / around myself
Now your rain / has rusted / our silver bars

I run my fingers / along the cool metal
And amber dust / sticks to my fingertips

You had me convinced
This was my home for so long /

It's hard, now, to admit /
I have always had
A secret key
Stashed away for emergencies /

I could have left your prison
At any moment /
But I was always too afraid
Of what you might do to me /

When I opened my cell door
And you actually heard
Your padlock
Hit the floor.

Acid Rain

Leave me alone

Amidst the midnight sands

I don't want your raindrops on me

Ever again

It burns like acid now
When you touch my skin

Maybe if I stop rewriting your fantasy for you,
My reality could finally begin.

The Playas

We were nothing more
Than a heavy downpour

That pooled
Into a temporary lake

At the lowest point
Of my basin

And I promised myself,
That day,
As we laid
In the Valley of Death,

I would never
Let myself again
Sink to
Such depths.

The Shallows

Her saltwater surged
Into my wide-open mouth
While her Arctic hands
Held my bruised neck down

Just below the surface of her sea
She eroded away
Every last trace of
Me

Sending
        Unwavering
                Waves
                        Of self-doubt
Until I could no longer see
The pieces of my body
She swallowed up
And buried in the deep

Hoping I would willingly
Dive into the undertow
Along her beach
Because that would be the only way
She could hold onto
A piece of glass like me

She figured if I saw
No way out
I would settle
For the bottom
Of her shallow sea

But I found it
Much easier to breathe
Once I shoveled her
Off my chest
And stood up

Off my knees.

Superbloom

Moving in Silence

The Sun is quiet
As she rises

There is not a soul
Unaware
She is there.

Fire Lilies

I burned down
Our house
By myself

So that from
The ashes
I could rise again
As smoke

Now as the fire lilies bloom
I wonder how
I could never see

This was your barren land
And I deserved
Gardens surrounding me.

Nostalgia

Once you learn
Nostalgia
Is nothing
But a liar,

You will realize
Real growth
Begins
Only after
The wildfire.

Overgrown

I used to think
You were protecting me

Keeping my body quiet
Behind the shadows
Of the desert willow trees

We were a sanctuary
Without the light

A haven
Without the peace

But now that you have fallen asleep
The Sun has finally come out for me

And there are thousands of wildflowers
Springing outward from my ribcage

Yet you still dare
To call them weeds.

Eden

Forgive
My feelings

They have grown
Far beyond
The garden's gates

Now they are
Out of my control

Though I see now
The truth —

I don't need to
Apologize to you

I am no longer
A piece of ripe fruit
That you grew

I am the Garden of Eden itself

I am the root.

Pollen

I was willing
To inhale
Your poison

Back when I thought
I did not deserve
To breathe

I was ready
To embody
Your sunlight

Back when I thought
I could have been the one
To help you grow

I didn't realize
Your sweet nothings

Had carried pollen
Into my home.

Dead Butterflies

You can't
Force
A connection

You either
Breathe
Life
Into every butterfly

Or you
Let them
Die

— There can be no in between.

Broken Window/Open Door

I've given up
On regret

For a window
Once broken,
No longer
Can exist

So a heap
Of shards,
We discard,
For there is nothing
Left to fix

Though it is thanks to you
That I learned to look far beyond the mist —
To scout for shooting stars
But to never bother making a wish —
They are just more end credits
We won't realize we missed

And it was you who taught me
How to contain the seven roaring seas
Without letting a single wave
Crash down on my beach —
And I now know how to break a heart
Without hearing a single
Shard of glass shatter beneath me —

So I will never regret
The scars on our arms
Or the bloodstains on our carpet

Or that I did nothing but watch
As you walked away
Leaving behind crimson footprints
In our driveway

Because now
The broken window
Of our home
Has become
An open door —

You can't pull our blackout curtains closed anymore.

Bloom

Into the dirt
With the old

Out of the dirt
Springs the new

Allow yourself
To bury the past

And your future
Will bloom before you.

Heliotropism

I am convinced
The wildflowers
Are gifted
With psychic powers

Beyond our comprehension
Beyond our third dimension

In my palms
Their petals
Spell out my fortune

Now the future
Is blooming quickly
Before my feet

And as I walk my path
I can feel the heat

As every desert sunflower
Finally turns around
To face
Me.

Soft Girl Spring

The wildflowers
Open up
To me

So I
Open up
To them

Our petals
Are soft
But our stems
Are strong.

Affirm

Feet in the grass —
I am rooted

Face to the Sun —
I am vitalized

Fingers towards the river —
I am fluid

Eyes locked on the sky —
I am something
Divine.

Phantom Pain

You had always told me
I had broken wings
But that you still loved me
In spite

He examined
Both of my arms
And assured me
They were
Perfectly fine.

Helios

If only I hadn't looked to the tide
As my one and only spiritual guide,

I wouldn't have kept coming back
To kiss the shore
After it had pushed me away once more.

I wouldn't have let
The phases of the moon
Control my every move,

But I always thought
The moonlight
Was the only light
That would ever
Be willing to hold me.

I should've known
It was refracted.

If only I had looked
To the Sun.

Clarity

He unlatched
A window
In my home

I never knew was there

The glass
Had been
Coated in dust
For years.

Rosewater

He pulled back
The desert thorn bushes

To reveal
A path
Long overgrown

Blood
Dripping
Like
Rosewater
From his hands

He would do anything
To help me find
My way
Back to land.

Ascension

Sometimes
This wild desert terrain
Seems too jagged
To traverse

Sometimes
This secret mountain path
Feels far too steep
To ascend

But I have love
Sewn into gentle hands

So we will climb
To the peak
Of this mountain

And I will still
Be holding on tight
At the end.

The Summit

Buttercups,
          Dandelions,
                    Tulips

Busy hands,
          Candied eyes,
                    Two lips

I taste
The summit
Of summer
Residing
In his kiss.

Life Preserver

The others open their mouths to speak
And anxiety tightens its grip around me

But when he parts his lips
He writes dimples on my cheeks

It's such a shame
He doesn't even see
The many ways
He has calmed these seas —

I was drowning
In the very saltwater
That poured forth from me

That is,
Until he reached out

And taught me
How to breathe.

Saturation

He says,
Flower
For me

Unravel —
Let me see

He says,
Your colors
Are brighter

Than anything
I have ever seen

Even in my wildest
Wildflower dreams

He says,
Come —
Saturate me.

Afterglow

My eyes were dark for years
And my shadow was navy blue
But a touch of his sunlight
Has made me a soft evergreen hue

And I'll never bruise blue so easily again
For as long as it is so above me
I'll soak in his ultraviolet waves
And grow yellow petals when he loves me

And I'll still crave the heat from his lips
Even with the fire I've been fed —
I'll still see him in every color
Although I am blind to his infrared

Because every morning that he rises
He gives my dark eyes a rest
And every evening as our sun sets
He leaves his afterglow on my chest.

Wildflower Nectar

My stomach
Is brimming
With butterflies

Wildflowers keep
Filling up
My chest

The honeybees
Never have a split
Second to rest

They all need
To know
How it tastes

To sip
A love
Like this.

Superblooming

I was once
The dirt
But I am now
The garden

I was once
The sand
But I am now
The ocean

I was once
Afraid of life
But I am now
One with the world around me

I was once
A desert wasteland
But I am now
A superblooming valley.

Grace

The live oak leaves
Are falling
And so am
I

Right into
Place
This time.

Notes

Several poems in this collection draw upon research from *A Natural History of the Mojave Desert* (University of Arizona Press, 2018) by Walker & Landau.

As Above, So Below

The line 'The landscape of his poetry was the desert' is quoted from *The Satanic Verses: A Novel* (Viking Penguin, 1988) by Salman Rushdie.

About the Author

Makaela Smith is a poet, artist, and nature enthusiast who has spent half of her life wrapped in the warm arms of Florida and the other half in the cool, evergreen state of Washington. She has a bachelor's degree in English with emphasis on Creative Writing from Western Washington University. After graduating, Makaela published her first chapbook *Ode to Summer* at the age of twenty-five. She currently resides in North Kitsap, Washington with her family and two cats, Sapphire and Haiku. To her partner, she expresses great gratitude as he has introduced her to a healthier definition of love and a new mindset that has motivated her to achieve her dreams of becoming a professional poet.